Pictures Never Taken

A Collection of Poetry and Thought

Marianne Burrow Gray

Order this book online at www.trafford.com
or email orders@trafford.com

Most Trafford titles are also available at major online book retailers.

Printed in the United States of America.

ISBN: 978-1-4669-7808-9 (sc)
ISBN: 978-1-4669-7809-6 (e)

Library of Congress Control Number: 2013901444

Trafford rev. 01/18/2013

 www.trafford.com

North America & international
toll-free: 1 888 232 4444 (USA & Canada)
phone: 250 383 6864 ✦ fax: 812 355 4082

This book is dedicated to my sons:

Donovan and Manuel

I am so proud of you both.

To my Husband: Donald, who got this started for me.

To my beautiful Grandchildren:

Jayden, Kaya, Judah, Eleyejah and Kanaan

Also, this book is dedicated to all of my dear family, those here and those passed.

God bless each and every one of us and thank you for always believing in me.

You, my family, are the reason and inspiration for my writing. Also to those

friends who have inspired some of these works, Love and God Bless.

Thanks to: My husband, Donald Gray
My sister, Ahna Yancey
My mother, June Herrmann
And to my friend, Nancy Foster
God Bless you for all of your help!

All artwork done by: Marianne Burrow Gray
Exception: Drawing of "Krystaleen Navybean" by Kaya NoRunner
All photos by: Donald J. Gray

Pictures Never Taken

A Collection of Poetry and Thought

Marianne Burrow Gray

SOME KINDA LOVE

Sea Cliffs for Me and You

Crystal blue skies,
Seagulls and butterflies;
Green-blue foamy waves curled
We have not one care in this world.
There by the sea, don't hurry.
Listen to the sea's thundering furry.
Crashing time after time,
Upon rocks across the shoreline
The fresh salty air clears out our minds.
Watching a pod of Dolphins, your hand holds mine.
There by the shore, bound no more
Nothing to do, no one to answer to
No hurry, no worry;
Just me and you!

Just Now, With Me

You have the money, I have the list
Who'd have thought it would come to this?
I'd grown accustomed to my way
It seems that now there is no time for play.
Only bills, to pay, pay, pay!
You know I say this with a grin;
Knowing all is right within.
No worries big, you make them small
That I may not bother much at all.
With any of those things, which before;
Pressed at midnight, knocking down my door
Just to make ends meet, what a chore!
One day soon, or, maybe later;
We will have riches at our table.
Oh, but lest I forget how
To see all the riches that we have now!
No, I cannot go back in time
To place you in that life of mine
I think this was how it was meant to be;
To find you now and here with me.

Sounds Good

Someone to hold my hand and be with me
Someone who wants to talk and tell me important things
Someone who's not afraid to say what's on their mind
And oh, so kind
Not afraid to hold me tight
Or put their arm around me
Someone who treats me like they're happy to know me
Someone I'd like to run to, bury my head in their chest
Escape; like a little child to a safe place.
Sounds good!

The Walk

In the cool December morning we walked along the path
Together, talking, sharing bits of our past.
You held my hand in yours. The leaves never looked so red, yellow and gold
Little did my mind imagine what that one walk would hold.
For as you held my hand, I felt a feeling start
And I knew, even if you did not, that then and there you held my heart.
I was a fragile thing then, yes, and I believe the same of you
We were both fragile then, but all of that would change too!
That walk was not here, nor on any place on this earth
That walk was in each other's hearts, and it gave us back our worth.
To be wanted and needed, to be recognized and desired.
Yes, this life had beaten us down and left us so tired.
But, for just once more my love
Let us talk
Hold hands
Live inside each other's hearts, and
Let us take the walk!

Mudslide

Mudslide and I'm goin' down
Slippery and wet, I feel I'll drown
I want to run…run…run
Don't want to hang around
To see this mudslide comin' down
I been down this way before
You got the answer? Please tell me more!
That strangers a' knockin' at my door
Tellin' me, to even up the score
Here I stand; I see no end in sight
And he's done give in without a fight!
I know how to love and treat you right
I feel I'm caving in, I think I might.
Mudslide, don't you hear that rain?
Raining so hard it puts my tears to shame.
All this water's gonna wash away
Any memories I thought I'd' save.
Mudslide chasin' me
Mudslide, I can't get free
Mudslide and I'm goin' down
Slippin' and slidin' I think I'll drown.

None but Angels

She brought her basket to him, laying it before his feet, her gifts, such as they were, for him alone.

And then he saw her, found her, like a child and lightly touched her head.

He accepted her gifts and he understood her intent.

There she rested in his embrace and looked upon him as her only friend. She wanted to look no further.

She became to him his only happiness and all of his hopes and desires rested upon her alone.

In all the wide world, their vision became narrow, until they only saw each other.

For them, nothing and no one else existed. And she wondered, was this wrong?

And he did not wonder at all but was content to leave it alone, just as it was.

They spent their days floating down the river of his veins and swimming in the pool of her heart.

They chased each other, both wanting to be caught, being voluntary prisoners unto each other.

There were no secrets between them and they cared not for this world.

He held her heart inside his eyes. She held his eyes inside her heart.

They wander together, forever now, and none can see them, save angels.

If I Were There

If I were there with you,
We'd talk the whole day through,
Or maybe we would choose
To let silence be our muse.
If I were there you'd see
The bright red side of me,
And with no words at all
I'd be there ere you called.
I would listen at your side
And in your arms I'd hide.
If I were there, not knowing
Down which path we would end up going;
Still, if I were there I would show
All those things you need to know.
All the things you'd ask of me
Would be yours to touch and see.
If I were there right now,
We'd make it through somehow,
And celebrate the day
That I was there to stay.

Borrowed Wings

If I were a bird with wings, this is what I'd do;
I'd fly across the ocean wide, just to be with you.
Landing at your doorstep, the magic would begin.
I'd turn right back into myself to meet with you my friend.
Knocking on your door my heart begins to pound.
There's city noise around me, but I don't hear a sound.
Then your door would open and I would see your face.
All the riches of the world, this moment can't erase.
Just to hear your voice, to see your pirate smile
Just to hold you in my arms would make it all worthwhile,
And so my friend, I say again, if only had I wings,
I'd gladly cross the miles, rather than only see you in my dreams.
For dreams can be sweet, it's true
But to hold, to touch, to taste they cannot do.
And so a bird I'd like to be,
Only a short while, to cross the sea-
All these things said half in jest, yet my heart it knows the test.
Borrowed wings take me to your door,
To be by your side forever more!
Yes, a bird I'd like to be, so I may cross the sea
That lies so wide from you to me.
Borrowed wings take me to your door
Borrowed wings take me to your door
Borrowed wings take me to your door
To be by your side, forever more

A Present

What a present you are;
Glory gold streaming from your heart!
All the things I never knew
All holed up inside of you…
Like a walk in the soft rain,
Like laying in the tall grass.
Looking up at the springtime,
Like opening a secret gift
That can only be seen with the hearts eye.
What a present you are to me.

Easy

As the falling leaves,
As the thin chill breeze.
As a morning walk,
As the way we talk,
Easy.

No explanation or expectation,
Here's where we are.
Here's how we came to be,
Easy.

To be there again
And just be your friend,
Would be… easy.

First of a New Year

On the morning of the first…I woke up.
The party was over and the sky was gray.
The morning of the first was beautiful, it rained!
I saw and I knew and I took it as a sign--
Strong medicine water from the skies…

The night of the first we were tired,
Tired like a blaze fading from the fire--
Into a tiny flame then into a smoldering ember

Still it rained on…run for cover?
We should but did not.
No, we remained instead.
You covered my head.
And there on Timber Lane
You rocked me in the rain.

WORDS OF THE
BROKEN HEART

Time will come

There'll come a time, yes, I am sure
When I won't see you anymore
Or hear your knock upon my door
Or beg for you back and ask for more.
There'll come a time, when I will rest-
When I'll be free of you at last.
When peace will replace the loss I feel
Where all my dreams will soon be real.
That time has yet to come
For I still fight to forget your love.
You have been gone for what seem years-
But time has yet to end my tears!
I still see you in the sun
See you in my work un-done
See you in the raindrops too
Yes, everything I see is you.
And I still see you in my chair,
And at my door and by the stair…
I feel you in my bed at night-
And in the switch that turns the light.
I feel your touch though you're not there
I see your face and feel your stare.
I know I've gazed into your eyes-
Though in the dark, a bad disguise…
I hear your breath
I hear your sigh
I hear your words
They make me cry.
I see you, feel you, and hear you still
Though you are not here and this is not real.
I've yet to see the day
When you'll be gone…for now you stay.
If only in my memory-
For my memory is all that's left to me!
There will come a time, yes, I am sure,
When I won't see you anymore…
Or hear your knock upon my door
Or beg God to have you back for one day more.

All There Is

People everywhere
Who can see their faces?
I can't see their faces.
Only you
Laughter everywhere
Who can hear the laughter?
I can't hear the laughter.
Only you
Rain everywhere
Who is keeping dry?
I'm not keeping dry.
Thoughts everywhere
Who is really thinking?
I'm not really thinking.
Only you
You…
I can't feel the sunshine.
I don't need a new rhyme.
I can't make it this time.
All there is…
Is you!

Casting shadows

I can't find a reason why it had to be this way
Why it couldn't last just one more day.
But you're not to blame, nor am I.
I've lost everything and my mind!
Lost it all, what is there to gain?
I'm laughing all the time to hide my pain,
Laughing so obviously, everyone's seeing straight through me.
I can't hide what this has done. It casts the biggest shadow on everyone.
Where do I go from here?
You can't give me any answers, you don't even offer.
And so I sit alone and wonder, the music pouring in and out.
I hear the song, I sing the words, and I'm left without a doubt.
But still it's there, when the music stops, when the song is done.
It shadows me again and I am the only one….so
To hide the tears, I smile.
To hide the pain, I laugh.
I can't find the reason why it had to be this way.
Why it couldn't last just one more day.
It's all the same, you're not to blame, I think …we're changing.

I'm Leaving

You know I'm leaving and when I go
I'm gonna miss you so much and don't you know
That I'll think about you and as I do
I'll remember all the good times I had with you.
Saying goodbye is not an easy thing to say
But soon I hope to say hello again.
I don't know, my feelings are everywhere
Tell me, do they show that I hate to go?
Any day now I'll leave this town behind me
I'll leave my number if you want to find me-
But you won't.
You know I'm leaving and when I go
I'll miss you so much, and don't you know
That I still love you and I hate to go.
I hate to go.

Alone

Walking alone I wonder if I'll ever be happy again
And when the summer night comes, I cannot face the moon.
It makes me sad and lonely, because I want to share it with you,
Then all the days are colorless, the nights are empty,
One after the other they fade, with unimportance.
Still I stand alone.

It Was You

I see the summer slipping away, shadows came to hide the sun.
My life so far could have brought anyone…It was you.
I'm here with fading time; you're there with fading dreams.
Time would see us together again it seems.
Maybe what we say, maybe what we are
The dreams we dream, our time so far…It was you.
Now a new season has begun,
I'll be waiting; knowing what will come…It won't be you.
You say we will always be;
But, I'm afraid to tell you what I can see.
It's not you, it's not you.
Tomorrow I'll see your face in the sound of this song.
Today I'll hear your voice and sing when it's gone.
We see all of their demands,
But we don't see the game in our plans.
We can't say
We won't live this way…
I know you.
I saw the summer slipping away, shadows came to hide the sun
My life so far could have brought anyone,
It was you.

They are for You

Can you see me, by my window
Watching the moonlight chase the stars?
Can you hear me, my voice a whisper
That tears won't let me talk above?
They stream silver rivers down my face.
No, my tears are not out of place.
I know that words will never do.
Please see my tears;
They are for you

Different Sky

I wake up every morning since I've been away.
I look out my window and see a different day.
Every evening I feel that something's just not right,
Then I step outside and see new stars in a different night.
Nothing is the same since I've been away--
Only my name- and a name is just a name.
I go out and try to have a good time;
But in the back of my mind, I think of what I've left behind.
I meet up with old friends who are different people now.
When they see me, they know that I too have changed somehow.
So, what can I say?
All I know is that I miss you so
And I want to go back to stay.
Daytime or night time, I don't feel right,
Then I finally see the reason why.
I am in a place that I don't belong…
Different style
Different love
Different sky

Because of You

Now the winds are up, just like the season we once knew.

They wisp through my mind to remind me of you.

The stars are out, but the moon is nowhere to be seen.

I know my tears will fall when he returns, from the sorrows he will bring.

Because I remember happier days and brightly colored memories,

But I'm faced with this shaking wind and not just an autumn breeze.

It whips me into reality…

Where the answer is so very plain to see!

I feel the way I do

Just because of you

Only because of you

Awful Truth

When first we walked along the path, talking, laughing, hand in hand
I saw no evil, I felt no wrong, and there was no thought of being damned.
And through your smile I fell in love and you fell in love with me.
There was nothing dark about our love, being apart was our only misery.
Although at times I saw your shadow side I pretended not to see.
Until one day your shadow loosed and made a fool of me.
Your words they stung and hit as darts;
My very soul, my very heart!
At last the truth had been revealed, the truth I had refused to see.
Our love, which seemed so perfect, was something not to be.
For there before my waking eyes, and in my ears your words a din
Made me see the awful truth, our love was naught but sin.

How Much Has Been Said

We've been through it all before.
We've let love fly out the door.
Isn't it a shame?
People can be so insane.
How much was said,
How much was done?
Too many harsh words for anyone
To survive
But let's stay alive,
Knowing we once had love.

THOUGHTS THAT

RIP THE HEART

WIDE OPEN

Baby Mine

Baby mine, oh, baby mine
Your hair has many tiny curls so fine.
Baby mine I held you close and kissed your face,
I kept your tiny hands in mine, though they held no embrace.
Your eyes open and sparkling as they look into mine
And I saw your tiny lips move as if telling me 'Good-bye'.
For you are gone to be an Angel my dear baby mine.
Gone away, baby mine, gone away
Gone away to heaven where I will meet you one day.

My Niece Jennifer

When you came into our lives
You were fighting for your own
There you lay, still and sweet
Tiny hands, tiny feet
We had so much love to give
How we prayed for you to live
And stay with us awhile…
Well, you made it!
Grabbing life from then on and running
You did everything!
From Brownies to softball and everything in between
Always ready to celebrate
Ready to win any fight
When Stockdale had Spirit Day
You always wore the Silver, Black and White!
You laughed with your cousins
Hung out with your brothers
You were a friend to many
A cherished daughter
You became a beautiful girl
Whom we were lucky to love
Our beautiful Jennifer Rose
When you left our lives
You were giving up your own
There you lay, still and sweet
At the gate of heaven, our Lord to meet
We had so much love yet to give!
How we prayed for you to live
And stay with us a while longer…

Eleven Years Past or Yesterday

All the colors that I see, all the songs that I hear,
All of the electric images I view…
Every single minute of every single day,
Everything everywhere is you.

You who I see in every shade of yellow
The birds out in the yard I swear they sing your name.
You who I feel in every sunrise…
That brings the sound of your voice down the hallway as you sing.

Yes; I feel your little push upon my shoulder
To tease me and let me know I'm getting' older.
I sit and watch the evening time shadows fall
They show me patterns of your smile across the wall.

Yes…I miss you every single day
I miss your voice, your funny ways
And yes, for all of this life I'll go on missing you
Until my reward comes…when you and I can start anew!

Outlaws

What we are today
Keeps us in our yesterdays
The way things used to be
The better you, the better me
What have we become, I ask you?
Did your dreams, like mine surpass you?
And did we ever have the chance to… do the things we should?
Are we just a mark in time?
With little reason, far less rhyme
Growing old our only crime, Outlaws!!!
When all is finally said and done
I know that I'm not the only one
Whose outlaw dreams dried in the sun, and finally blew away…
Because I know that you too saw a star in a lonesome night
And wished upon it with all your might
Wished and hoped and dared believe, that one day you'd hold the dream.
Alas, it passed you by!!! And so it goes for you and me…
But there is one thing you can hold onto fast,
Of all your present and all your past,
Remember always what is yet to be!
And never forget what you've meant to me.

Me and Joe-Joe, When I was Queen Mary

You used to know everything…Or so it seemed

I thought that you were great without a doubt.

Whenever you talked to me, I would pretend to know what you were talking about.

When you would leave, I'd rush around trying to learn everything about what ever topic you had discussed.

That way, the next time I saw you, I would be able to say; "Hey, I knew that all along"

You treated me like someone special.

They treated you as if you were the devil.

Maybe I was a bit naïve to believe that you knew everything,

Or maybe it was because I was in fact, a child?

Now that you're gone, sometimes I sit and think…

It was never good enough, that I thought you were good enough.

You wanted recognition from another place.

Of course you did, I was just a little kid,

And I could see it on your face.

I wonder if you know now, how hard I tried to let you know

That you were a very special person in my life?

Since you been gone it makes me realize how people come and go,

In and out of our lives

Guess nothing's changed here, no, nothing's really changed…

Except, now that you're gone,

There's no one to hear my song.

TO MOM FROM 'JEO'

For Mama

You were there when as a lad
When I was sick or hurt or sad
Through all my triumphs, big or small
Through all my glories, you shared them all.
Always you were the one
I told my worries to
One by one
I always felt as if you knew
Because I shared those times with you;
Those early days, just you and I
Not gone for good, just set aside.
I'll see you when we meet again
For you and I are still best of friends.

My Regretful Heart

In my risky heart I dare,
Feeble of mind, I walk a dim path.
Never quite understanding why
What then is left to say?
Here I am, fallen…fallen…fallen
Like a star from the heavens.
Sitting alone, chin in my hands,
I feel like a little child.
Is this the way it's supposed to be?
Gone…Gone…gone, are all those days,
Never to return again-
Lost…Lost…lost, to me-Forever,
 All the time I could have spent,
With you my sons…
What was I looking for?
What did I need?
Why must it all be repeated again and again?
Let me not stumble and let me not fall
Never to get up again!

Hark! Herald Angels Sing; Auld Lang Syne

(In Memory of Herald "Hal" Yule)

We heard music, yes; the music drew us in. Little did we know the chance we took as we stepped inside your door- how could we imagine it would be life changing? Witty, engaging, and such a deep pool of knowledge; I knew that you were someone with many layers. Reminding me of a pyramid filled with many chambers, corridors, rooms all filled with golden treasures. Warm and inviting, like a teacher who dearly loved his subject. No fever-pitched slickness of a salesman- NO. You were giving things away, things like; knowledge, pride, understanding and reverence, just to name a few.

Quick wit, big hugs, lots of class and love. Each of us can tell a story, our own story of how you touched our lives. In the end, remarkably, it is the same story we all tell. For you belonged to each and every one of us. Thank you, for making us all feel special. Thank you, for sharing yourself, your time and your wealth of knowledge. We will miss you and hold dearly your memory, until we all meet again: For auld lang syne my friend, for auld lang syne.

THE GOOD THE BAD
THE NOT SO SANE

That Game I Play

Maybe, just maybe, I've met my match. You'll have to teach me to read between your lines.

I heard that, I kept that, I stored that….upstairs in my secret room.

Who are you? Where do you come from? Is your reality less than what you wanted it to be?

Now, I can write all night long, and I can teach you to sing my song.

I can let your lean-to be my castle. But, your eyes, well, that's another story. I ask you, let me dance upon your heart, I tread lightly.

You see where I come from. The place I am escaping from, you see it…you see it, don't you?

Do you want to know me? Do you want me to listen as you tell me your life? Then will you bother to hear mine, or will it only bore you?

Is it you I'm looking for? Is it me you've waited for?

What do you believe? Won't you tell me? Is there an idealized image of me in your mind?

What have you told yourself about me? Is it anything I could believe in too?

Try as I might, I never get things right. I just play the game and mangle all the rules!

Holding Hands with a Stranger

Some things strike me as funny…how odd things become as we grow old.
Once you ran the household.
Everyone minded, everyone obeyed the rules
You accumulated bunches of things…Pretty things-
Some things you need- really need
And others, you just want.
Once there was a house full of children;
Or maybe only one or two;
Oh, they knew not to touch this or that.
They knew which were the fancy dishes.
Then one day, there you are, not even dead yet…but close to it.
Or, oh heck, you say you might as well be!
All of your things, pretty things…Keepsake things, garage sale things
Rag-tag things or maybe even diamond rings.
All of your Things…Odds and ends
Are all divided amongst all of your kin.
And you, well, you have made a new beginning.
In an old-folk's home, there in a chair….Holding hands with a stranger.
The stranger who may become your best friend!
The one who'll be there beside you until the end…
These are the things that strike me funny.
And though you are too proper to say it aloud, you think 'Well, aint this a bitch?'
When suddenly, these words come to your mind….'No ma, you were.'

Passion

Passion, what an awesome feeling

Passion, what a powerful master

To have it, some would cross great Oceans.

To feel one moment of passion, one would dare the highway.

When you walk a lonesome road

And all that was once warm, grows cold inside

For Passion, one would take a treacherous ride

Stumble through deep darkness.

Lay aside our old dreams

Perhaps lay aside our beliefs!

For passion we lust….the unknown.

Crawling on all fours, we seek for passion like water in our dry desert lives.

We stop progress in its tracks, to feel passion

Just the thought that we may have some, fills us with insane desire.

We lose our vision if we have no passion, and we lose our vision in search of the

same.

If you have it, you are lucky indeed

If you have it not, a pity!

Rebellion

No excuse!
Rebellion
Temptation
Being robbed
Keeping the door unlocked.
Knowing not to-but doing it anyway.
I have no excuse;
I know better!
Looking for mercy;
Being worthy of none.

Contagious

Where did I go wrong?
Why didn't I see the turn in the bend?
Where did you go wrong?
And how long ago did all of this begin?
Insanity is contagious!

Strong

These words I hear they give me strength;
I won't be left behind, I will go on!
If my favorite number one, is not called
I will go on to the next.
And so on…until they do call it.
I can choose to be alone.
But I never have to be.
I am not a monster.
I am from this planet.
Maybe it's my way of letting my broken heart turn to stone.
Never to be hurt again!
That is why I have become so good at '*good-bye*'
And 'hello'
But, I'm not too good at '*stay*' and '*forever*'
Though stay and forever is what I always thought I wanted.
Nevertheless, I have had to learn the hard way.
I will be face to face with this storm.
And I will be strong!

Safe Keeping

I can remember the dark walls in your room.
Your eyes the only light, like a glowing ember.
Sometimes shining, glistening with teardrops
Not meant to be seen.
Your heart accidently revealed to me.
The words that you rehearsed;
I now forget them.
The words, never meant to be said, slipped out;
I now remember them.
The part you were acting
I now forgive.
The part you couldn't help playing
I now recall.
The piece of your soul you gave to me;
Do not worry, it's in safe keeping.

Hiding in the Grass

What's all that smoke?
Is your house burning down little girl?
Tell the truth;
What is it you want and can't have this time?
In your mind, in your dreams, with your mouth
You say; "Everything is alright."
Your hero hides in the grass girl.
He's not there for you,
But, you won't admit it.
Never mind, a whole life time won't change a thing.
You'll be looking back at yourself like in a dream.
The one you love hides in the grass…
What's funny is; nothing you have can coax him out.
Not your desire, not your pout,
Not your 'T n' A', nothing!
Even if you had brain one, he would not notice.
Yeah, your house is burning.
Burn alone, burn alone;
It won't kill you, but, it might turn you into a freak.
You can live with that.
You can live with him.
You can see he's hiding,
Hiding in the grass!

Silence

That's OK, I can take it
Though I seem like a little girl
I am growing up.
I see things now, I've never seen before,
It makes me wonder why I let so many things slip through my fingers.
Silence is a weapon.
It always defeats me!
It tears at my very soul and leaves me bleeding.
Silence tells me lies;
And I believe them!
It scares me and I let myself be afraid.
Silence is a killer, and if I let it, it will murder my heart.
And I won't be able to love anymore.
Then and only then will the silence;
SCREAM!

Untitled

I've been walking.
Listening to my footsteps fall.
I've been talking;
Listening to my voice recall
I still think about you.
There are days I do so well.
I still go on without you;
There are days it hurts like hell.
You were no good for me.
And you were the best thing in my life!
I know I'm sounding contradictory;
But, you know how wrong I'm right!

Brain Pain

Memories of life gone by, learning to pretend we've not been here before.
Surprise, wonderment and longing, Gray matter like gray rain;
Fills our brain
Brings us pain
And knowing!
Lock boxes, that hold the keys to all our parts;
Makes us stop
Makes us start
Makes us break our heart;
By letting others steal our goods.
You know no one ever could-
If you never let them!
Thinking, knowing, longing, growing
But never getting any bigger!

A Piece in Time

Having had a bad life, starting on the day he was born in prison.
Just up until he was spit out by the 'system'
Straight out, into the 'generation of Peace & Love'
While years before, 'Hobos' were looked down upon
Here he was face to face with a new kind of hobo.
One with a hippie smile and long hair…
One with a flower and a body to freely share!
Everything was free!
And then he knew that the planets had been aligned just for him.
Yes, the devil himself dipped in his wicked finger to paint the times just right.
And how was anyone to know that an album of white,
Would hold the key
To the horror-movie summer that would be?
In all of his life he had never had so much good luck!
In all his tiny life he had never had so much fun.
Fun-fun-fun in the California Sun
Yes, he had found a piece in time
Tailor made for his crazy mind.
His own bloody playground of 1969
That had become the psychedelic backdrop-
The perfect backdrop for one
Yes, in 1969 didn't Charlie have fun!

Someone Else's Dime

You have your vices; smoking, drinking, whoring and the like.
You have assorted drugs, only the free ones.
Standing there in your cheap shoes, with a dirty finger on the mic,
You swear you were in the band.
If we look hard, we'll see your name there on the LP.
You say you played keyboard…or was it guitar?
You came from somewhere…
Every time we see you, it's from another place!
We don't laugh behind your back,
Man, we're laughing in your face!
Someone else always pays your way.
Sometimes they do it, just to make you go away;
But, you never do!
You're like unclouded water in a clear glass.
We can see right through your ass.
Now you've got someone else believing your lies.
And it will all go down on her dime.
Until she finally sees through your disguise;
Pose pretty for the latest donor to your toss-up lifestyle!
She doesn't know how lucky she is, you'll only be her nightmare for a while.

The Hollow Man

Someone you fancy quite a bit bore a hole right through your head.

He told you lies, disguised as truths and you chose to believe what he said.

Young and so impressionable he knows your kind so well.

If he can't bend you, he knows there will be another and another.

He has to fill his kingdom and so he haunts the halls,

Chasing tiny minds so fresh so new and so ready for alternative thoughts.

He tells you with his sweet voice, that there is- *no heaven or hell.*

He licks you as if you were honey and you faint beneath his spell.

To believe all he says empowers you.

You feel strong and smart and free.

To be hard as a rock to rise above all standards

He's taught you to turn your back against the *norm.*

The root of all, is his voice and it envelopes you.

You lay in it and wallow in it.

To hear his voice, is your only desire.

He wants you to know that *nothing* is sacred

And no one is holy, this you must know.

Once he's got you where he wants you, he leaves you swooning on the ground.

He, that once filled your every waking hour and moistened all your dreams,

He's left you to find others who will hear his voice

And who will swallow his lies.

Others, who will embrace his false wisdoms,

And swim in his sea of "anything goes"

Nothing is angelic he says.

But he looks like an angel.

Nothing is sacred he tells you,

But his voice sounds so holy.

There is no right or wrong he whispers softly.

In his absence you begin to wonder.

There are times that you almost forget the sound of his voice.

Did he ever even exist at all?

That's when he reappears!

"Don't leave me now my young sweet thing; it's you I've ever loved".
He lulls you back with music sweet and flowing dreams of erotica.
You wake in the morning, still wrapped by his arm.
Believing he will not leave again,
Drowsily you trace your fingers across his skin,
Watch him as he's sleeping, you feel warm red run down your fingers
And flow across his shoulder, this doesn't seem to bother you.
He breaths deep in his sleep, is he dreaming of you?
His eyelids are half open; his eyes glide back and forth.
You smile; can this be what they call REM sleep?
What could this beautiful creature be dreaming of?
Ever so quietly, you dare to look into his half open, sleeping eyes.
And much to your horror and surprise,
You see the hollow man.

Who's running this show?

Sometimes I stand my back against the wall.
Sometimes I stand, facing, yet guarding myself from the fall.
I can look into your eyes and dance upon your heart.
You can take me to heaven and you can tear me apart.
There's only one thing I want to know, tell me, who's running this show?
Is it you or is it me, is it fate, could it be?
Sometimes I tell you everything I feel inside.
Sometimes I tell you things to make you run and hide;
From me-
Maybe I can't see the forest for the trees.
Maybe I'll only recognize the things I choose to see;
I see you-
When I think I've got it all figured out,
You act out of role and plant a doubt.
I gave you the script, you know every line.
I wrote it, so how is it your show? Why can't it be mine?
There's only one thing I want to know;
Tell me now, who's running this show?

Missing a Nightmare-Sometimes

Makes me laugh, the thought of you,
It makes no sense that I ever loved you.
Still and all, there are a few small things
I miss about you;
Like a bird would miss its wings!
There we sat, in any restaurant
No need for me to order, you knew what I would want.
You never let me stir my own coffee, you did that too.
One sugar, three creams, not two-
Your arm always at my side,
And no matter where or when;
Your hand always held mine.
In a movie theater, driving in a car;
Like a bat outta hell; but never very far.
You could answer any question that anyone posed to me.
And you made damn sure everyone knew you belonged to me.
Makes no sense, after all you put me through;
After all the dread and hurt, how could I miss you?
Tell me, how it is and how I didn't know;
That when I left you, I would ever miss you so?
You took my years, you took my youth
You took my health and my sanity too!
Princess in a box, more famous than 'The King'
Your tiny hummingbird that you kept tied to a string.
You never 'just' loved me; no, you poured yourself out upon me like gold.
'Baby you're my reason for living' Not a day went by that I was not told.
And sometimes, in the back of my mind I still hear those words today.
Just a whisper, just a passing thought;
Like a taste or an aroma that the morning brought.
'I'd die without you' will sometimes play in my head,
And there are even days that I'll recall just everything you said.
To own something is nice enough, to own someone, not the same.
I was your possession and that is how it remained.

You never let me go and you would scare me so I would stay.

And all of this because; you didn't want me to go away.

Standing beside you I would try to hold onto any reason that kept me there,

While always in the back of my mind I knew I was with you out of terror and fear.

Makes me laugh, the thought of you,

It made no sense that I would ever love you.

But, you finally caught me, by getting lost inside my eyes.

All of our time together turned out to be pure lies.

You took from me just everything and everyone I loved.

Until my prayers to the Lord were finally answered; yes, He heard me from above.

Leaving you was hard, because you had become my drug.

But to save my life, and others, I had to leave you, the thing I thought I loved.

For a while, it was hard and I felt like giving up.

I thought that without you, there was no use in going on.

I told myself that no one would ever love me like you did.

Now you were gone.

I don't know how, but I made it through.

Now I have everything and nothing, since I escaped you.

I know what it feels like to be loved, or so I think.

I try to break the measure of it, but I cannot.

I was everything to you, all you needed,

And all you ever would!

At times I think I'd be with you still, if I could.

But, you were impossible, irrational…not right…..in the head!

We had some good times,

You made me feel like a million dollars.

Though I knew the truth…..I was just a damaged wreck.

You saw me through your desire eyes, and so you didn't check.

I was special to- _You_-

And; that's what got me through!

It got me through…

Makes me laugh sometimes just the thought of you,

It made no sense, _and perfect sense_, that I ever loved you.

THE BROKEN CHILDS THOUGHTS

The Best Costume Dad Ever Wore

My father was never drunk on Halloween. He never owned or wore an actual costume per say, but, he was *always* in disguise make no mistake about it. On Halloween our dad went as a *good and sober father*! He always bought us the biggest pumpkin on whatever block we happened to be living on at the time. He always carved the biggest and best Jack-O-Lantern to set on our porch. He and mom would always rig up something spooky to pose by our door. Mom used a standing floor lamp for a body with coat hanger arms sticking out towards the oncoming trick-or-treaters. On the end of each coat hanger arm, she added yellow Playtex gloved hands. Then she dressed the lamp in a sheer flowing night gown that blew each time the door was opened. It was extra spooky with a huge hat tied under, what looked to be, a faceless horror.

There was so much laughter in our home on Halloween. Dad had fun, *real true* fun. Fun, without drinking! How do I know this? I saw it and I felt it; we all did. He enjoyed picking out the biggest pumpkin and carving it into the best Jack-O-Lantern. Dad enjoyed giving out candy to kids. He would sit on our porch with a huge bowl of candy and smile as the kids walked up yelling "trick-or-treat!" That was how he got his biggest kick. The kids would step up to fetch their candy and see this handsome, smiling, dimpled man with a bowl of candy and when they got close enough….suddenly to their surprise and sometimes horror, Dad would quickly push out his false teeth leaving them sticking half out of his mouth. Some kids dropped their treats, screamed and ran away. Others, in shock, stood stalk still, their eyes wide in disbelief. More than a few boys would say "Do that again mister, do it again". He would stick his teeth out for them a few more times and then give them candy and tell them to get going. He had to be ready for the next set of trick-or-treaters. Most all of the kids caught on, or, were told by their friends, and they always came back to make sure they got candy and one more look at the crazy man that popped his teeth out at them.

My dad laughed so hard, he really laughed. You can't laugh the way he did unless you mean it, unless you feel it. It was a real honest laugh, over having a real honest good time. Our family was together. We had fun; we laughed together and played around. We counted candy together and even shared some of it. Mom always made our costumes and we always won 1st or 2nd place in the costume contests. But, the best costume every Halloween was the one worn by our dad. On Halloween he went as a good man, a good father and husband. It was the best costume dad ever wore. Halloween was the happiest day of my life….every year. Nothing bad ever happened on Halloween. Nothing ever will.

Down By the Seaside Sifting Sand

What is missing? I asked myself as I sat there by the waves. Looking down, there lay a tiny sand dollar in the palm of my hand. Pebbles and a pile of shells lay nearby, as I knell sifting sand. A song kept playing inside my head, a song they sang, the waves roared on, - calling my name.

That was such a long time ago. Where has that little girl gone, I ask myself now? She had so little but she knew so much. She knew way too much. Things that she learned constantly filled her thought. Things she had seen made her worried and frightened. Somehow at that young age, one thing came through as most important to remember. *A man is life.* Without a man, what would make life worth living? To be without a man to love, was an impossible thought. Somehow, even though she was very young, a child of no more than 5 or 6 years old, she had already planned what she wanted to be when she grew up; *a wife and mother.* There was no thought of any type of alternative. She had learned that nothing mattered as much, nor could be compared to, being a wife and making sure that she put The Man first in all things. The children, well, every woman had them. Having children wasn't anything to concern herself with, since they would look after themselves', while she, of course, would look after the man. In a nut shell, that was the sum of life. Life, as she knew it, life as she saw it and as she learned it.

The one thing she thought she had down pat, to get and keep a man. Then, to make sure that man was treated as the King he was, the one thing she knew she was perfect at. Well, that was the one and only thing that drove her down her life path ......to no end....... to nowhere.......to near death.....to the gates of hell. When would it end she thought? When she finally found the right one of course! The one who was as wretched as her dad was, but, unlike her dad, for her, he would change. Change from a bad man, into what? ....why, into a knight in shining armor of course!

That was when it would end. Yes, it would end, when she cast her pearls before the swine that would appreciate them.

What is missing? I asked myself looking at the tiny sand dollar I held in my hand. There by the sea side sifting sand…"*Marianne, oh, Marianne, Oh, won't you marry me?*
We can have a bamboo hut, and brandy in the tea…"

Orange

The sun is hot,
Our hands across our eyes
To block its blaze
     At night, A thousand neon lights
     Through the orange haze
We run, until we're out of breath
And so thirsty
We laugh, we cannot stop
And we're dirty
From head to toe, with city smog
Our heads with radio, Become a fog
     Sometimes we're brainless, sometimes too aware
     Of our surroundings
The daily, nightly soundings
Of an endless pitch
Of mama's bitch…about dad's bottle
     And us alone…Almost grown
Through the orange haze
Our wistful gaze,
Onto the future…Of our past

Untitled

We missed the star, it passed us by.
No, we let it pass us by.
Illusive? No it was not!
Just slightly out of our reach.
Ah, maybe if we had been taller…

PAINTINGS
PAINTED WITH A
WORD BRUSH

BROWN AND BRITTLE

The rosemary doesn't get any sun.
The myrtle grew so wide
With Zech's apple tree to the other side
The rosemary doesn't see the sun.
The birds fly by
Across the myrtle so high
The sun beating down…
Rosemary in the shade, wearing a brown and brittle crown;
Standing stiff and dead in the ground
Wearing her brown and brittle crown…

I Day Dream Again

Tiny River running far below
 Mountain top thoughts
Drown out the sound of any water
Like a blue-green ribbon across the package of Gods beauty
Tiny river running
I daydream yet again!
 Oh, to grab and embrace all this beauty, but how?
When I can't even grab and embrace my own backyard!
Daydreams, be gone!
Only let me see each dawn
Where ever you Lord, feel that I must wake….
Well, that is where I will be!
Just to live and to feel it,
Only keep me from my daydreaming.

Ghost Town Shanty

Most of the glass panes are intact. But the wooden window panes are getting old and split. The paint, a shade of green, is flaking off. The wood is splintered, and the front door is long since gone. But there's a screen door, torn here and there. It swings back and forth in the wind. It makes a clap, clap, clap sound. Dust upon dust, upon dust, upon dust, sits at the tiny kitchen table. It sits upon plates and inside tin cups. The old stove heats nothing, but houses cobwebs. There's a speckled tin coffee pot atop the stove; its lid with hinges rusted open, forever yawning in the small one room.

Against the wall, a shelf hangs askew by one nail over a single bed of iron metal. Under the bed, a boot, a man's left boot - the sole so worn there are holes with bits of cardboard showing through. The air is dusty, old and sad. No one has lived here for many, many years. There's a bird's nest in one of the eves of the low roof. A lizard perches still upon a brick by the door, as if listening intently to the clap, clap, clap of the screen door as it swings in the breeze.

Sitting in September

The sun is going down in a sky so blue, over a field of tall brown- yellow grass that waves with each breeze. I sit, hidden, listening….to birds, crickets, rustling blades of grass and the creaking of Eucalyptus trees nearby. The sun sets ever lower, making the slip of view above the grass a blaze of gold. Every nocturnal animal and insect picks up an ever quickening pace in their orchestra to the coming dusk. When I see the flighty moths dancing along the grass, I know it's soon time to go. They move as if marionette puppet strings are directing their wobbling flight. Soon it will be full on night. But before I get up to go, they pester me by bouncing against my face to leave a smudge of their brownish silvery wings against my cheek. No one has taught them to give a proper kiss good bye! I smile at the awkward moths and wonder why they can't be as graceful as the butterfly. See you tomorrow, to sit in September.

Earth Song

I am the morning dew and behold the branch I sit upon
I am the silver stream that rushes by before the dawn
I am the evening breeze. I often hear my mother call
But I am almost grown and it is fall.

I must sweep away the leaves and hear their branches cry
No time to stop and comfort them, for they themselves must die
I am the mountain that proudly gazes over all the land
I am the shining diamond crystals of snow and of sand.

I sit behind unmeasured stone and watch the daylight tire
As it strains out its final sigh, *to last*, its sole desire
I am the shadow over the stream made by the lonely tree
No bird, no man, no animal are near to stay with me.

I am the peace, the hope, the dream
The lonely tree, the silver stream
When you're looking at my face
I'm free and light of sorrow
But come my friend and kiss me quick!
For I am gone tomorrow

Brave Boy

Brave boy, who walks alone
In the woods, that he has known.
He stops along the path to play,
In the drifts of leaves, at dawn of day.
Kicking the mound of leaves, listening, he laughs.
The gold, red and yellow all crunch, make a shy deer jump past.
Stuffing a few leaves in his pocket, he finds a stony place, beside the creek.
In the chilly autumn dawn, he kneels to have a drink.
A noise in the wood catches the boys' ear.
 It's the elk he's often seen when he comes walking here.
The elk gives the boy a look of recognition, friendly yet stern.
The boy doesn't move, but makes sure to quietly nod; good day in return.
Kicking a pine cone, along he goes, picking up a crooked stick for walking with,
Then, stopping to pick a wild rose that he'll take home as a gift.
Now the boy's reached the brook he loves to cross
Knowing its rocks are slippery and covered in moss
But oh, they are fun to balance upon.
As he carefully crosses, slippery noises echo in the dawn.
Soon the boy finds the other side of the path; back home he must return.
He quickens his pace, for now he can smell the dead leaves start to burn.
The smell of burning leaves, reminds him that father rose in early morn.
Being the only son, he knows that all the chores must soon be done.
There's so much to do, all of the animals want feed before the sun.
Oh, but the sun's been up now for a while, this thought gives the boy cause to smile.
He takes a deep breath, to face the day, to do the things he knows he can.
He's ready now to leave his boy self behind, for the rest of the day he must be a man.
When he finally reaches the kitchen door,
Mothers' bread is made, her kindling lies upon the floor.
Before the hearth, she sets the table
With butter sweet and sugar maple.
The boy reaches into his pocket, the crunchy gift he hands to mother
The red and gold and yellow leaves, that along the path he'd gathered.

Mother smiles at her boy and bends to kiss his head

But the boy, with hand held up, bids her wait instead.

Yet another gift he has, mother kneels beside him, and as she's waiting there

The boy reveals the wild rose he picked; and with a kiss he places it in her hair.

Father walks in from milking the cow, happy to see ready, the tea and biscuits too.

A pat on the back he gives the boy,

Father; *Now son, how about you?*

Boy; *Well father, I rose before dawn.*

I put my little boy clothes on.

I walked and ran all through the woods

Enjoying the dawn as much as I could!

I played in the leaves. I saw my friends the Elk and Deer.

I gathered leaves and a wild rose, and now father I'm here!

Ready to face another day

I'll go put my little boy clothes away.

Thank you! For giving me the early dawn to wander free.

I'm her now, and well ready I'd say

To be a man for the rest of the day!

California Without

The hot air of summer, late August
The smell of horses and leather saddles, tall trees and mosquitoes
Pine needles crunching underfoot,
Sierra Nevada day-
The sticky sweat that catches the sand
The coconut oil, tropical smell on a salt-watered body
The sound of the waves crashing against the rock,
Central Coast summer-
Then there's the fall, the only fall I know…
The orange, the yellow, the gold
Never hot, but, never too cold,
The California Harvest time!
Blending into winter, from yellow-orange to Christmas red,
The trees, the gifts, the ever so slightly cool nights
Here on the coast.
Springtime, green time, a field of color…
A hum of insect noise to serenade you and hold you
In the cool green grass that closes in all around you.
With a butterfly field and a grasshopper mile,
With a laugh, a tear and a smile-
From desert to ocean view, the California seasons are remembered
But lonesome without you

Once upon I time I was

Once a princess, tiny and fair,
Eager to venture anywhere;
All I would ask is that you would meet me there.
Once so brave and able to venture free,
Out to the very edge of my realm I would flee!
No second thoughts, of any danger I would find;
Only that which lurked in my mind-
I never listened to advice
When given to me once or twice.
I ignored all that unwanted news.
And only heeded what I would choose.
Bravely I declared; *'I am small, yes, that is true…*
It does not mean I'm not like you!
It will not stop me from anything…Anything I want, or dream!'
I pushed myself to where I may,
through darkest depths, or brightest days.
All the while hiding the fear, that within me lay.
I cry now at what has become of me, no, I cannot lie.
How shall I break free, to once again touch the sky?
To balance what I know to do
Yet, remain to myself true?
How fragile I am feeling now
Though I will make it through somehow.
With faith that moves mountains, and keeps my path straight
To do what must be done, and not hesitate.
Only that I were- what I still long to be-
Do you remember the tiny fair princess upon your knee?
Safe in the forest, safe from this storm;
Damn the lightening, damn the noise!
To feel your grace surround me tight;
To know you are with me all through the night.
To hear your voice that lets me know

You are with me still and will not let go.

Deep in the forest where I long to be;

Where safety ever surrounded me;

Where leaves of gold and red and green;

Light on the path you made for me.

The path you laid so long ago.

For a princess who might happen by.

Whose touch you treasured as if gold!

Whose passions mirrored in your eye!

No knight, no king, no common man-

Can save me now from what I am.

It is in my hands to turn around,

For alas- my kingdom has fallen down…

To my former glory I will return, though it may take a bit of time,

To be that princess you once knew in that far and distant time.

In that far and distant time

Our Last Dream

Here in the stillness I feel the cold of the night.
I hear the sound the cold makes no need to go outside to feel or hear it
It creeps in, seeps in through the walls
There's a defiant chill.
Yes, I can feel it straight to my soul.
What's about to happen, do I really want to know?
I see a rainbow in your eyes, in your smile
I will take them, if only for a while.
I hear an echo of 'good-bye', though I try not to listen.
I can hear it sometimes in the wind
I know that if my heart breaks, it will surely mend.
It has before…
Let's close our eyes and dream, and learn to dream, in our own way.
Let's promise each other to dream both night and day!
 And in our separate dreams, we choose the colors we want
We choose the songs that we want, we dance our own dance.
And given the chance …we fly!
And I, in my dream, will not fear falling.
And you, in your dream, I'm sure you'll be soaring.
Clear out of sight!
Then I will wake up to the song, the last dream will linger on.
And I will miss you when you're gone.

Times I Dreamed to Live In

As a child I dreamt of living in a distant time
Where women wore dresses long and church bells chimed.
Where the ladies all gathered for noon time tea
With tiny teacups held upon the knee.
All talked politely and wore large bonnets
While some ladies read from books of sonnets.

The men folk dressed fine on Sunday afternoons
Some smoking pipes and others whistle tunes.
They rose when the women folk brought them iced tea
And no one went indoors until nigh after three.

In the evening round the table Father said grace
Each child ate all their supper and left not one trace.
When supper was done the family gathered round the fire
Uncle John would tell stories of which no one would tire.
Until finally Mother called them all off to bed
And made sure that each child's prayers had been said

The mornings would bring a handsome young man to the gate
He bowed low before the ladies after securing his steed to the stake.
Oh how handsome his voice did sound, as he asked ever so politely if he might
bring
Mothers young Ann to the Ball this upcoming spring-
In response, there with the children all 'round, young Ann could be seen
With her cotton apron crisply pressed and her paisley dress all in green.
With a shy smile upon her sweet face and her cheeks a flush
The children giggled and mother hushed.

Mother looked the young man square in the eye
And before away on his steed might he fly-
She yelled for father, her voice so shrill…
Plop! The young man fainted just like a girl.

Father rushing out to see such commotion
Helped the lad up and for his horseman did motion.
He let the handsome young man escape with his life
While under his breath whispered: "Son, you don't know my wife"

Young Ann did complain at her mothers' strictness
Father laughed but then quickly minded his business.
Mother tugged young Ann by her ear all the way into the house
Each one held their tongue, tiptoed as soft as a mouse.

Oh such fine days to be living in
Strictness and rules and nary a sin
Ladies long dresses and gentlemen saying grace.
Bonnets and tea time and smiles on each face
Oh these are the times in which I dreamed to live
Way back in the day when I was a kid.

Painting a Picture for No One but Me

I sit at an old wooden table. Sunlight streams through a tiny paned window. You know, the old fashioned kind, with little hinges so they open outwards like a door. The walls are thick. This place is old. I sit here with a cuppa something warm. The window is open a bit and a breeze, breezes in now and then. The flowers outside the window are so tall. Its greenery so thick it makes a hap hazard garden of sorts. No dragonfly can resist, no hummingbird dare leave this beautiful place outside my window. Now I've known this place a long time. Although one might say, only inside my mind. As a man who sits in prison and never ever is released, I sit and dream of what my escape may be. Although sickness is the only thing I wish to escape from.

Some people dream to be rich! Oh, I am no different. But not so as to have those fancy things, no, only to be free to have those simple things which I long for. Riches for some, mean treasures, and to me, mine are treasures too! Riches; which I know would make things a bit better, and keep me here on this earth a bit *longer*. Sometimes riches do come in handy, even if you need only the smallest of things. Mine would never be wasted on glamour or glory, but, perhaps to buy more flowers for my garden! Or even a new tea cup or two for fine company who might stop by. To sit with me at my old wooden table, to look out the tiny window and have a cuppa and a laugh or two. Feeling the breeze come through my tiny window, looking out onto my garden… that hap hazard paradise to dragonflies and hummingbirds, and me with good health at long last!

And so until then, I paint a picture for no one else but me….a tiny cottage, a wooden table, a tiny window that looks out onto a glorious garden, and me, without sickness, yes, well at last….and there I can grow old and smile and laugh and do the things I could not do before, things so simple, but, so simple that money can't buy…

From a Dead Kingdom into One Living

I stood upon a desert plane. My view was the wasteland of my home.

The dry hot breezes blew. Blew away the dreams I'd known.

I longed for something I once had. I missed the green and rolling hills.

And longed for things I never had! Desires deep in my heart not filled.

Daring was I, to take the chance, and set my foot upon the path.

Into your kingdom, chance brought me there.

Deep in your eyes, a winding stair

I climbed, I climbed…And not carefully!

But, without fear, I climbed willfully.

Once inside your eyes…..my keep!

I will not dare to rest nor sleep.

Green your kingdom, no deserted plot

As mine had been all death, dust and rot.

Here am I now, just at your command.

Your eyes they have saved me from my barren land.

For you saw me there and did not turn away.

But, smiled kindly and bid me, come be refreshed and for awhile stay.

Return? I will not to all the hurt and the fear.

With you I smile and shed no tear.

With you, for you, I am at your call.

You saved my life. You have my all.

The past is gone, is blown away…

Here in your kingdom I will play.

Within your embrace, I will rest for a time,

Where I am yours and you are mine.

Please know I am thankful, even for a small moment's pleasure,

And that my grateful heart, is yours forever!

Monterey

The day is clean; a tiny sharp breeze is in the air.
And in my mind, I long to be there!
By the bay
To hear the sound of the bells far away-
The creek-creek-creek of rope against the dock side,
To hear the laughter from the carousel, and the seagulls cry!
The Irish Pub with its green lights that give the foggy street a glow.
And the Irony that there are no sardines to be found on cannery row!
The irony that there is no place that I can go
To escape this feeling and this longing inside
And no way to hide-
My love for you that grows stronger with each day.
Monterey

Krystaleene
Navybean

Krystaleene Navybean wore bright red boots
That could not be seen.
When she walked her dog around the block,
All the neighborhood stared and gawked.
And when she went to school,
She looked barefoot as a rule.
But to the wonder of her class,
Krystaleene could run through glass
With never so much as a cut or gash.

When autumn time came, the children liked to jump through the dried leaves.
Right there in bare feet Krystaleene could be seen!
At Halloween the children all went to trick or treat
With Krystaleene in her costume and only her bare feet.

The winter time was so much fun;
With sleigh rides and snowmen and snow hills to run.
The children all called for Krystaleene to come play,
And she ran out to meet them with her bright yellow sleigh.
Krystaleene Navybean was dressed warm like her friends
In mittens and snow suit and wool cap on her head,
But while everyone else sported warm socks and snow boots,
Krystaleene could be seen with pink polished toenails so cute.

In the summertime when the asphalt was hot
While Krystaleene jumped hop scotch, her friends could not.
For though she looked barefoot just like them,
The hot black top never burned her skin.

What a mystery it was to one and all
That Krystaleene Navybean seemed to wear no shoes at all.
Not one of her friends and neighbors ever did know
That Krystaleene wore bright red boots that never did show.
But all of Krystaleene Navybeans family knew very well,
For her boots had been passed down from her Great- Grandmother Nell,
And where Nell got them from, she'll never tell...

RANDOMS

Right here!

Worlds there are out there...
Here am I
Welcome home, where have you been?
Looking, ever searching,
Not getting very far
Your own backyard
Your own front step
Your key fits the door!
Where grass is green
And
Birds ever singing
If you are older
Don't despair
You are not yet old.
Look...look around you.
Worlds there are; right here.
Right here!
Where you are...

Past

No need to sit and complain about the young
Because the young will be here until they're old.
No need to sit and talk about the way things used to be;
Those days are gone and won't ever be back again.
Once we were young, do you remember?
How we hated and loved to be the topic of everyone's' conversations.
But the past is just that…
It's past
We live now.
And we try to grow old with some sort of dignity
We put out of mind any wrong we may have done.
And believe in God, that we are forgiven!

Money Can't Buy Health

The weeping willow
The pessimistic
How long did it take you to come to this?
Pollyanna all are we
Until we hear the stories three.
Her version, his version and the truth…
Worst case scenario, on such a beautiful day.
Dying for what all your money can buy
And dying literally because all of your millions cannot buy it!
Life
Your very life
When your number's called
Cannot be bought at any price
Doing some praying are we?
God Bless….God Bless!

Fallen Friend

He said each hair of our head is counted and he knows each time a sparrow falls
Today I saw a sparrow dying in a parking lot
I said a prayer for him
I did what little I could for him
I don't think it was enough
I wished I'd never seen him there it hurt me so
Christ cares for us; he cares for the fallen sparrow
I told the Lord that I expected to see that bird and every other bird I've tried to
keep from dying
I told Him…That I expected to see them all again in heaven
And I believe I will

Maybe you're afraid

Maybe you're afraid of what I'll think of you
Maybe you feel I'd never understand
Don't you know that you can never be happy, if you can't just be yourself?
Don't lie, don't do a cover up
Say who you are and don't give a damn!
Are you to blame for the things you feel?
Didn't God create the man?
And if he did, and if he cares
Don't you hope He will see you through?
Or will God condemn you, like the world does?
And if they judge you here, will He still need to judge you there?
You are who you are, you'll know in the end...
For now, maybe you're afraid to trust me.
Maybe you don't know I'm your friend.

Untitled

The sun came out today, after being gone so long
Without a reason why;
But all too soon he pulled a clouded veil across his face,
So he wouldn't see me cry
…Because I hurt someone

When We Saw Dylan…Bob That Is

He smiles so wide-
There's a great big smile on his face!
Eyes wide open…
But he's lookin' into space.
Yeah he must be a million miles away.
Maybe remembering somethin' from another day
Smiling as he recalls what he had to say
Laughing to himself as he sings and plays.
Just lookin' at him in his leather vest,
I must have forgotten I was all grown up
I figured there were no new scenes,
Knowing I would never give this one up!
He just looked out at all of us-
He just never saw any of us!
He just would not stop smiling
And not one of us was what was makin' him smile!
Yeah he must be a million miles away
He's remembering someone from another day
Smiling as he recalls what she had to say
Laughing to himself as he sings and plays.
Aint it great to see Bob Dylan?
Must be great to be Bob Dylan!

Nureyev

Delicate, silent wings
Only sounds of music
From the silver screen

Watching you soaring like an Eagle
Yet gentle like a dove
Earth's laws cannot hold you, tie you down-
Nor chain your love.

Nureyev, please dance for me
Violent, ecstasy!
Leap for me with your boundless steps
So light they seem!

Drifts of snow so light
Falling stars so bright
Dance for us tonight-
All the world is waiting!
…waiting, Nureyev

Adam

"Moon up high" is what you said
Bright blue eyes, golden head
Wishing you were mine instead!
You lucky boy, how great for you;
To have my big sissy as your mom
And to be my nephew!

For a Friend

My friend is feeling lost and low, Lord help him, for you can.
His future looks so dark, the present a demand.
I am just a friend of his, I cannot give him time.
Tell him that you'll help him through; give him peace of mind,
Make him see the good in every day he spends,
Let him understand the closeness of his friends,
Send him the love he needs, Lord set his spirit free.
He's changing, finding out that the world's not all it seems to be.
He's changing…make it easy for him.
I am just a friend of his, I cannot give him time.
Tell him that you love him…give him peace of mind

Two Club House Blues

#1 The Bell Rings

The bell rings. It's not the front door.

The bell rings. It's not the school bell.

The bell rings. It's not the alarm clock.

The bell rings. It's not a bright idea come to mind!

No

The bell rings. It's time to recharge the cell phone.

#2 Waiting for Eric

Get on with my own thoughts as quick as I can.

Never mind complete sentences.

He's something to ask.

He's something to show me.

He'll be round in a bit.

So, here I sit…..waiting for Eric.

SOME RECENT PASTS

Pictures Never Taken

Pictures never taken
Memories in my heart
Days in sunshine blazing
First school days torn apart
Gathering seashells
Posing on a rock
Arms around each other
Fingers as if locked
All the blank and nothingness
All that is not there
As I sit here crying
Gathering some stares
Everything we cannot see
But all in what we took part
The pictures never taken
Are now memories in my heart

Cisco

I am famous in your eyes.
I could never be replaced in your heart.
You know me,
I know you.
You're always with me.
To think you may not always be here breaks my heart.
Somehow though, I think we will be here and together
For a good long while.
I'm not always right…
Who knows?
But, you are a part of me, my friend to the end.

Cherished

Irreplaceable

Sweet

Crazy

Old friend…

Apologies

I saw my dog Cisco talking to a brown mouse that was sitting on our garden fence.

I don't know what they had to talk about, but, when they both turned to look in my direction,

I took it as my cue to close the curtain. I didn't want to appear the eaves-dropper.

I wondered if the mouse was scolding Cisco for his sometimes rough behavior.

Or maybe Cisco was making his apologies for biting the squeak out of the mouse's family.

When last I looked out the curtain, Brown mouse had gone and Cisco was eating the tall grass and pushing over toadstools with his wet nose.

Another Happy October

October came and went
Many happy days we spent.
We will not mention any day
That was less than, how do you say....Perfect!
Anything that matters most
Was that all of our family was close.
Even those far away,
Seemed a little closer those October days.
Pumpkins grinned
Candy eaten
Oma in costume
Children greeted.
Warm cider on a full moon night
Come now my sons, it's only right-
Let us toast to its beauty, now over
Cheers! We'll see you next year October!

Husband

If you feel that all is useless,
I will show you that it's not.
If your efforts loom too large above your head
I will show you that none of your efforts are in vain.
If you are tired, tired of the days and the nights,
I will let you rest on me.
I will be here for you,
As you have been here for me.

My Mother- or- Jackie O with a Black Eye

Full of fear and doubt
She wore an overcoat that oozed Class!
A contradiction of fierce pride and dark shame
She was as fragile and delicate as fine crystal glass.
With a tongue so sharp and strong it could set your world ablaze.
She wore her halo perched just above her horns!
She was not born that way,
But, she was made that way.
Molded and crafted into a fine ball of knots.
Shaped by the gods to be sure!
But, battered on the insides by the insane and the dark-
These days… my Mother,
Still Jackie O, of course!
No black eye.
She's removed her horns and set aside her halo.
And at long last- she's just class,
Wise as an Owl, stronger for the ride-
Her serrated tongue dulled to a soft humbleness.
But, still sharp with wit and wisdom!
Just my Mother
And all for Jesus is she!

One Day I'll Write a Book

One day I'll write a book. It will be a kind of scrape-book, with pictures and captions.
It will be called: "AM I HAPPY?"
-As a question-
And, by the end of the book anyone who is reading it will know that I am…Happy!
And anyone reading the book will realize that it has nothing to do with money
…
But, lots to do with Pumpkins
And freedom
And green grass
And trees
And a country house
That has a boysenberry pie cooling in the window.
With a nearby corral where my Burro's nose twitches at the smell of it!
Where my dogs chase dragonflies around the yard
Where my husband makes wooden toys in his shop
Where we can go fishing anytime we choose…in our own pond…
Oh, I can't wait to write my book!
Until then, *Am I Happy?*
Always!

Life is Good

Don't you just love it when happiness is just as dramatic as sadness?
Fulfillment just as ominous as emptiness
Euphoria as addicting as depression…even more so!
If you have to wallow in anything, why not wallow in joy?
Pass the pixie dust, not the Kleenex,
Cut me a big slice of life
Hold the caution!
Weeee Life is good!

Days that Money Can't Buy

My front door, lot's of flowers on either side
Birds singing, chirping, cooing, calling to one another
The smell of lavender on a spring day
The smiles of my dogs, my faithful friends
Memories and dreams
Dreams of days to come
Dreams in Heaven, forever happy!

Ode to Our Red Oak Tree

Tree I love you in the summer time
When your leaves a deep green
Give me shade sublime.
Where Papa hung a tire swing-
Where still we hear the laughter ring
A tree house held for two brothers
No girls allowed, not even mothers!
Winter, with your branches bare
Outside my window give a frigid stare
As if asking me; *'What's cooking there?'*
Christmas cookies the shape of trees no less!
My Oaken friend, need you guess?
Spring time tree, your leaves a tender light green
On which dewdrops glisten and sheen
In the early morning, suns first rays
Easter time through sunny haze
Upon your branches where Grandma hid
Easter baskets for the kids
An Easter egg lay at your feet
Brightly colored and ready to eat.
But tree- you know I love you best
When the world gets ready for a rest
When your leaves change color from the green
With your golden red- orange you smile at me.
You stand at my window and once again
As if asking; *'what's cooking there friend?'*
Pumpkin cookies for the grand kids
And cookies shaped like autumn leaves,
For me to frost and them to eat!
I only need to copy there
My friend beyond the windows glare
For all the colors that I need
I see in you, my friend my tree!

Peace of Quiet

And this little piece of quiet I was afforded.
To have met you, means the world to me.
No door in or out, we're just here.
This piece of quiet I was given by a friend.
She asked me for a favor
Unbeknownst to her
She gave me one.
Lately I patter around doing what must be done
Constantly it seems.
But now, this piece of quiet all my own…
There is nothing demanded of me.
I can only sit and contemplate the leaves
As they rustle in the breeze.
The sound of the train
As it click clacks along the tracks.
Why must I hurry back and leave this piece of quiet?

Leave it behind

Sometimes you look back
Sometimes you look back
Sometimes you look back on all of the years
On all of the fears,
On all of the tears,
That you've cried, cried, cried
Oh come here child; and rest in my arms,
Forget all the harms.
They are past now, over and gone, gone, gone, forever.
So don't you look back, don't you look back to peer,
Upon all those old fears,
Upon all those old years, gone by…
No, you just turn your head,
Look up instead.
Close the door,
And say your-
Good- byes, bye, bye
No you can't change it anyway
You can't go back there to play
And no matter what you say
About it now
It's all just words,
Wasted words…
So be the free bird that you see in the sky.
Oh come to me child,
Rest your head awhile.
Leave it all behind.
Think of me sometimes.
Leave the past for good and all behind.
And then take off,
Yes take off -
And fly
Leave it all behind
You just take off-
Take off and fly!

No More Front Door
(New Orleans Katrina)

What do you do when you can't go home?
If you do, there's nothing to go home to...
A few brick stairs, maybe.
Water, water everywhere,
And everybody sinks.
What do you do when all you've ever known is-POOF- gone?
Never mind knocking, there's no more front door.

Dancing With My Grandson

What a happy night it was with our campfire glowing,
Celtic music was flowing-
There on a beautiful starry night,
Round the campfire burning bright…
I danced with my grandson!
Five years old and forty-five are we
Beneath our moon lit campsite, dance, did we
Jayden said *"I'll teach you to twirl"*
As we danced I felt like a young girl
No longer a grandma- "Grammy M'
Just dancing in the moon light, me and him-
He told me; *"My feet are little just like yours Grammy M"*
"And that is why we make perfect dance partners"' I answered him.
As the music played its Celtic stories in song
I explained them to him as we danced on.
And just as I finally ran out of breath…
"Hey Grammy M, let's take a rest!"
And rest we did, round the fire once more,
A cup of coffee and Chocolate S'mores
I know there will come a time when Jayden will no longer be-
In any kind of mood to dance with me!
Until later, much later-
At his wedding, yes, perhaps we'll dance then
And on my 99th birthday we will dance once again!
Jaydens' feet will be bigger, mine will still be small.
But, that won't bother us at all-
Oh there is nothing quite like it in this wide world
Than to be dancing with my grandson, who taught me to twirl.

Thanks Be to God for Birds!

The birds sing and chirp happily outside my door. A soft spring rain brings a gentle sound that gives them cause to sing. They sit in a little line upon my fence. Their feathers wet. They have a shower. Some are dark with black rings round their necks; they are Black- throated Sparrows. I feel so lucky to have almost every type of Sparrow arrive in our yard eventually each year, from the Song Sparrow to the Lark Sparrow and all in between.

Present are the House Finch, so colorful and so many! They are tiny noisy birds with Red heads, Yellow heads and my favorite, but not as common to my yard, the bright Oranges!

And the Dove as big as a small Rabbit, soft tan and creamy, like coffee with lots of milk. The beautiful Mourning Doves huddled together under the rosemary bush. They are here every year and make my garden their home. This year there are two couples! They try to share the yard and are so kind to each other as well as to all the other birds. I can see that by their constant presence and laid back temper that this is their home. This makes me smile and praise God, how blessed I am to have them honor our garden by making it their own!

Here we also have Rusty breasted Robins and bright yellow and black Orioles, and when I am oh so lucky, the Western King Bird! This year how blessed I was to see one at the top of our bare Red Oak tree. The sight was beautiful. The King Bird sat on one of the top-most branches, the brightest blue sky the backdrop as I sat for near half an hour listening to its "dawn song". What a miracle to me as the sun was just up enough to show the bright blue sky. I was wishing I had my camera, but I was frozen there in the swing just looking and listening to this King Bird and didn't dare go inside to fetch a thing.

Today though, the Sparrows and Finch are content to sit atop the fence; being gently rained upon. Once the rain stops, they huddle at the feeder and splash in the bath. I love them all--even the Black Birds, and the drab little browns, various shades of coffee and tea. In spring time there is a constant hum and bustle because all of the birds sing, play, and chase each other in the grass and into the pink daisy bush. They perch just hidden inside the Rosemary and at the cue of one, all at once, they start popping out of the Rosemary and seem to rush the feeder!

In the summertime, I see Hummingbirds darting in and out of the Lavender and Lemon Tree.

When the yard goes quiet and I see all of the peaceful birds in the garden scatter, that's when I know, and it's not long before I hear the loud "ka-aac-balk" of the Blue Scrub Jays, or "Biker Birds" as I like to call them. The Finch, the Sparrow and even the Doves get out of their way. The Mocking Birds try to imitate the Jays in their bravado, but not as effectively. The Jays come in pairs and soon they take over the yard. No more sweet singing or warbling , not a chirp or a *coo-coo*, all of the other birds take to the high branches and sit silent to watch the Scrub Jays in action. Jays take as long as they please and if a brave Sparrow or Dove dare show its head; quickly they're squawked at and chased away by the bossy Jays.

Blue Scrub Jays, they are loud and proud and can be bullies. They wear their colors proudly. They fly in and take over the whole yard. Once they have screeched enough, bullied enough, and made a great mess of the feeder, they leave. Never do they stay long enough, not nearly long enough. Only for a while do they grace my garden, making it their vacation home, or maybe more of a watering hole or a truck stop! They are so arrogant I know, and despite this fact, they are so blue I find myself hoping that they have left me a small token of one of their blue feathers. How I love to collect them.

I am always sorry to see them go. But when they do leave, I soon hear the familiar sweet chirping and singing. I see my garden back to normal again; there along the fence the little red, yellow and orange headed Finch chirping happily. Out pop the Sparrows from the branches of the Rosemary. The Doves take their place sitting in the grass getting some sunshine in between the gentle rains. All is as it should be and my fine feathered friends, happy and relaxed, keep me company once again.

CELTIC INSPIRED WORDS AND THOUGHTS

Annie's Mum

Oh we love to dine with Annie's mum,
And how we love to drink.
On any day at any time
That woman's at the sink.
She's always somethin' cookin'
And never short on ale.
Oh we love to be at Annie's mums,
To drink and tell tall tales.

Oh Annie's mum, Oh Annie's mum
She doesn't have one penny.
We don't know how it is that she
Can feed us lot so many.

Oh Annie's mum, Oh Annie's mum
She hasn't got no teeth.
But we love to see her smiling,
As she serves us up the meat.

Where does she keep her ale?
For we know her larders bare
We don't know how she does it
But she doesn't seem to care.

Oh Annie's mums always singin'
And speakin' of days long past.
We sing along and listen to
The old dears' gums a-flap.

She's got no kin left to her,
Not a husband or no lands.
By the grace O' God, we do believe
That's how she fills her pans.

She's always somethin' cookin'
And feeds us one and all.
She's round and fat
And to beat all that,
We've never seen her gnaw.

Oh yes we've seen her drinkin'
And way into the night,
Sometimes we hear dear Annie's mum
As if she's had a fright.
She gets to screechin' and screamin'
'Bout hearin' the Reapers call,
Cause when Annie's mum gets tipsy,
She can shake a banshee's bones.

Sometimes she says she's not long for this world
And she'll meet us at yonder gate.
Then she'll laugh real loud, slap her knee
And ask us what we'll eat!

Oh Annie's mum has no shortage
Of beef or pork or fowl.
She's plenty of taters and cabbage
And an ocean full of ale.

But she hasn't got no garden,
Or a rich gentleman at her call.
All she's got is nothin'…
But one brown mangy dog.
She likes to call him Butchie
And he's nice and fat and round.
Annie's dog wants for nothin',
Like ol' Annie he feels sound.

Oh the lot of us we love her
Each gray hair upon her head.
We love to hear her singin'
Afore we're off to bed.

Oh Annie's mums the best ol' girl
For reasons known to some.
She'll feed ya and she'll drink ya
Until all your ails be gone.

We don't know how she does it.
It's life's true mystery.
But if you look for all us boys ta'nite
You know just where we'll be!

Oh we love to dine with Annie's mum
And how we love to drink.
On any day at any time
That woman's at the sink.
She's always somethin' cookin'
And never short on ale.
Oh how we love to stay at Annie's mums
To drink and tell tall tales.

The Smile of Ireland

Once upon a time, I stood and felt the cool night air,
Away afar in Ireland, that land so green and fair.
No story book could ever tell an adventure such as mine
To stand upon the Cliffs of Mohr and smell the salty brine.
No love poem could ever capture the love within my heart,
While I stood in awe at St. Kevin's Church as I knelt to touch its hearth.
Few could read such words of faith that Irelands Saints posses.
Few could give a soul pure peace, solitude and rest.
For a song no man could sing, no whistle blow, no drum nor string
Can deliver music so fine
As the tunes I heard throughout the towns of that green Isle so divine.
Once upon a time, I stood on the doorsteps of Ireland.
No novel could tell the tale, nor fiction capture, nor poet describe
The feeling within me that still lingers inside
As the brightly painted doors that never hide
The smile of Ireland

Highlands

It matters not the rain!
For this is why I came
To be set free!
In this rain, by this sea
In these mountains and in these trees
Where for years I've dreamed to be.
Smokey gray mist rises over the rocky hills with slabs of green.
Rolling, rolling, rolling on, as always I had dreamed.
The fog is so thick and wet as I walk along the path.
I feel enveloped, none can see me and this puts my mind at rest.
The gray sky turns blue and then bright with sunshine!
The weather ever changing makes the Highland rhyme.
Upon each Mountain side, as if streaming down a craggy gift,
Flow the silver ribbons of water that sparkle at each cliff.
It matters not the rain!
For this is why I came
To be set free!
In this rain, by this sea
In these mountains and in these trees
Where for years I've dreamed to be.

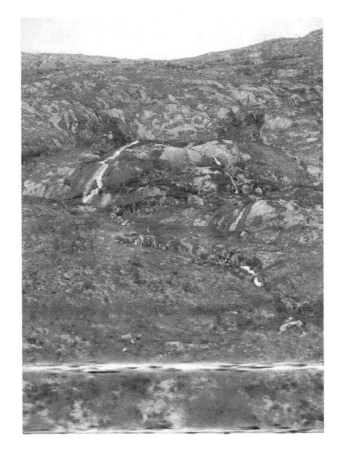

George Square

George Square had vertigo
But I was standing still.
Standing still
Standing still
Thought I heard a voice
But it was passing in the Square.
Thought I caught a glimpse of you
But there was no one there.
I kept waiting for someone to say
I kept waiting for someone to say
I kept waiting for *anyone* to say;
"Just stay"

Night's End .....Glasgow

Jury's Inn, Jamaica Street. Tourist…..ME…I think we were on the 7th floor or was it the 10th? The hotel window wouldn't open much, so, I had to squish through and kind of hang out as far as I could to see the street below. In any case, I could see the Clyde. I was only in the room at night time. The whole of the days were spent seeing, walking, running or riding along in a Glasgow rickshaw.

We'd get in late, after a pint, singing "The Auld Canal". Right away I'd hurry to the window to hang out again…..because even back in the hotel, I didn't want to miss a thing. I didn't want to see a hotel room at midnight or one in the morning. So, I kept my head poked out to see the lights twinkling along the Clyde. To breath the Glasgow air, to see and feel the "foggy dew"…..I stayed that way, just kind of hanging out the window, until the street lights went out across the street….until every last sound died down and all was quiet.

Only then would I leave the window and turn to my bed.

William Wallace

The chill wind blew and struck his plaid to dance as a flag
As a symbol for all to see
His sword held high
Screaming the battle cry
That his people shall be free!

Robert Burns

Who were you,
This icon we celebrate?
Whose grave inspired Wordsworth!
The voice of the common man… perhaps.
The Elvis of your time…Yes!

Ceilidh
(kay-lee)

A night to remember
Swirling, twirling, loud without fear.
Jayden dances with a drummer, Kaya perched on Papas shoulders.
Oh how proud I am to see them here!
Friends and family happy, laughing
A wee bit of fun
A wee bit of meat and a wee bit of drink
Music, pounding and strong
Music, soft as springtime rain
Music that none will soon forget, and in our hearts remain.
Ceilidh, a wicked good party night!
Young babies and old great-greats
All welcome, all as one. All of the same tribe!
Pipes and drums chase any bad memories from mind
Music that made us dance.
Made us shout out loud and cheer!
Making this wicked good Ceilidh night, a night we'll always hold dear!

Busy Dublin or the Citizen

I saw you standing there alone in a crowd. I too was alone in that crowd. Strangers' voices filled the air. Pigeons landed here and there. No one looked at me. You probably thought no one looked at you. I was invisible amongst the population, like pigeons-- invisible and ignored. You were not lonely; I could see that. I was not lonely, just happy to finally be there. You I envied, because you didn't have to leave. No, this was your town; you were at home. It didn't matter which was your house, but only that your address was here. Not mine, no, I was the visitor; my address far from here. You did not know that I observed you, weighed you in my mind. I could see you were content.

I wanted to be like you, to have a place not only to call home, but to feel home when I said it. You had that. Even if you were standing alone in a crowd....with people coming and going, walking the shops or taking care of undone errands. You stood alone in a crowd on a sunny day in your town. Yes, even the pigeons that lived and gathered there were at home. They lighted and nuzzled right in the middle of a high traffic walk- way to catch a nap in the sun. They landed where they wanted and slept where they wished, without any fear of being trampled underfoot. Yes, even the pigeons felt content; nothing pressed or loomed upon their day! They were like you, at home.

Then I caught myself, remembered who I am, a visitor, just a visitor who would have to go ...home? No not home, just back. I had no choice, I had to go back. Taking one last long look at you, the citizen, I sighed and walked away.

The Celtic Lands

For many years, I dreamt I'd go across the sea so wide
When chance allowed, I took that chance, to see the other side.
Far beyond the dreams I'd dreamed, its beauty stilled my mind
And being there surprised me more, at the peace my heart did find.
Even though so far from home, I knew this land so well
For it was just as near to me as from childhood I could tell
For all those years my mind would go, to wander o'er its hills
There I stood, just as I had dreamt, and held it at my will.
Yes! I'd be there now
If chance allowed
I'd go there once again.
I'd bid farewell to those I love, a new life to begin.
Yes, a new life to begin.

The Village Named; **Shimmering**

Candles glow in the window, the hearth is burning bright.
Laughter from the Tavern, with friendly smiles that cheer the night
Lit by stars and moonlight mirroring the sky,
Causes sparkles on the river as it goes rushing by.
Fire bugs twinkle in the evening, like tiny fairies that flutter in the trees,
Magical and lovely they dance along the breeze.
Lanterns light the path along the way to home
The Lane that's called Holly-hock is the lane that leads to home.
Up in the tree those round lanterns; are just the Hoot Owls eyes!
Making the night more magical hearing the night birds cry.
This tiny village, these nights with family and friends,
Even all of the animals and all of their kin
The living glow of light made by insect, bird or man
Keeps our village warm and bright, with happiness at hand!
That is why we see happiness and joy in every little thing,
For every night is brightly lit in our wee village Shimmering!

ME AND TONY

Bonnie and Clyde

I'd sit in the passenger side of Dad's
Old blue Chevy truck.
I was Bonnie Parker.
You were Clyde Barrow or C. W. Moss.
When we needed a driver.

I chewed a fake cigar that I made
Out of paper,
You'd talk about our next hold-up.
We got real mean and wouldn't let
Any other kids in the garage.

"Stick 'em up, nobody move!" you'd say

"Give Clyde you bubble gum Raymond,
Or we'll blow your head off!" I'd say.
…and he'd give you the gum, or he wouldn't play!!!

Daydream Believers

I was Davy.
You were Mike.
Sometimes we would trade off
And be Micky or Peter.

Cardboard guitars,
Hairbrush microphones,
Day glow peace signs,
We would sing our lungs out!

I'd fake a great British accent.
And you'd wear a wool cap.
We were great,
We were groovy…
We were the Monkees!

Office

You brought the blank checks to me
I was the secretary,
You were the boss.

I sat at the end table,
That was my office desk.
I typed and typed,
My typewriter, an empty oatmeal box

I stacked the papers,
And filed them away
The game we played,
On a rainy day

Matchbox Cars

I smoothed out the dirt.
You made all the roads.
I placed pieces of green bushes
Near the rock garage.

The cars went up and down,
Back and around.
A whole city block of matchbox cars,
            Matchbox garages,
            Matchbox houses.

Mod Squad

I was Julie (sometimes Pete)
You were Link.
Dime store hand cuffs
Stuffed into the pockets of our bellbottoms.

We arrested ever square we saw!
We were cool, we were the Mod Squad.
Two by four Harleys,
The washroom was the jail.

We arrested our poodle, Coquette,
A milk-bone dog biscuit was her bail.

Army Man WWII

I smeared dirt on my face and clothes.
You were the; "General Tony Burrow Sir!"
I was; "Private First Class Marianne Burrow Sir!"

I carried my stick rifle.
I stood at attention.
I hit the dirt at your command.

The rock grenades were flying.
I got hit; I was wounded, or worse!
You always got a Purple Heart…
And you never died.

We crawled along the backyard fence
We dug a trench to hide in.
I packed saltine crackers for us to eat…
And milk in our canteen.

Mom would always come out;
"Don't forget!" she'd say,
And give us a chocolate bar for "energy"
Just like Daddy had in WWII.

Halloween When We Were Kids

The night is cold, but we're in a sweat,
' what do you mean you're not ready yet!'
'Hurry up, Hurry! I don't want to be late,
The costume judging starts at eight.
Besides all that, there's trick-or-treating,
Just think of all the goodies we'll be eating!'
Up and down the streets we go,
On every porch the pumpkins glow.
Yells and screeches in the night,
Another glorious Halloween night!
'I'll tell on you if you kick my bag.
Don't go to that house, she's an old hag.'
The house down the street gives the biggest candy bars;
Hershey's, Milky Way, Baby Ruth and Mars…
We run so fast we're out of breath,
'Have we gone down this block yet?'
The fog is thick; the air is still now,
Far away a faint spooky howl.
Down each street the jack-o-lanterns glow,
Nearer and nearer to our house we go.
It's getting late. The voices die down,
Ghosts and goblins are going home now.
A ghoulish scream here, a whistle there,
The last trick-or-treaters are getting a scare.
Counting our candy as we stumble along,
Another block it won't be long.
'I'll trade you my Slow Poke for your Black Cow'.
There's our house, we can see mom now!'
She's on the porch checking for us down the street,
Calling and waving, *'did y'all trick-or-treat?'*
Our jack-o-lantern still grinning on the porch,
Its familiar glow our welcome torch.

'Did you two have a happy Halloween?'
'Yes mom, yes, and the best we've ever seen!'
One last straggler comes for candy at our door;
We give him some of ours, Mom ran out hours before.
It's the end of another Halloween night,
And there's a tug on my heart to see it take flight.
Sadder still is the way I feel now,
Lonesome and sad and sorry somehow.
For I realize now, that never again,
Will I run up and down those streets with my friend.
Or throw a costume together at the very last moment,
To win first prize, who would have known it?
Never again will Halloween be,
The way it was for you and me…
For all of these are but memories, sweet memories of mine
Of when you were eight and I was nine.

SPIRIT TRUTH

Free

The Lord set me free!
And I want you to know that my soul is free.
Now watch it soar!
I want you to see what's happened to me.
Like never before
There, away on the sand
Like food from the land
I see my freedom.
Come, don't be afraid to take His hand.
He's always loved you;
It's all been planned.
So open your door
And you too will feel His love
Like never before!

You Are Mine

Lord everyone keeps expecting me to live my life the
Way they think is best for me.
They can't understand that since I found you
And because of You
I've found my sunshine through all these rainy days.
I love you Lord, much more than I can say!
You make me happy; the mere thought of you can make me smile.
No one else has the words I need to hear.
Those who know so much, but don't know you
Their words are empty,
And I long for them to finally know you.
I realize Lord that I will never, until Heaven
Finally know you myself.
Everything is brand new
Just like you said it would be…and so…
I hear only you…in everyone who speaks.
I see only you…in everyone I see.
I touch only you…in all those around me.
I speak of only you…to anyone who'll listen…
I live just for you…when no one's looking,
And you are mine…and the whole worlds.

Who Are You Waiting For?

I am waiting for Jesus, who are you waiting for?
Here we are Lord, hand in hand
 Ready, waiting for heavens command;
We long to hear the trumpets blast
Angels proclaiming that you are here at last!
The thunder claps and the clouds roll away!
Praised be God, our Savior comes today!
All we peoples of the earth look up to heaven
Waiting, wanting to see your face now forever!
And so each one asks the other-
Who are you waiting for?
I am waiting for Jesus, Jesus Christ our Lord!
Amen

In Spirit and In Truth

There by the Sea, watching sea birds fly,
Listening to the sound of the waves crashing and the passersby-
There in a garden sitting upon a stone,
Watching the cottontails in the quiet when alone-
There at the window, when you're watching the rain
Turtle doves duck for cover and the wet taps at the pane.
The relative quiet only broken by Gods creatures' great and small
No doubt or query as to the fact He made them all.
There in the sunlight in a boat upon the lake
No hurry, no worry, no looming mistake.
Nothing can take you from Gods spirit and truth.
When we worship Him in our hearts, where ever we be…
Where we see all his beauty, there His Church will be!
 In our good times and in bad
When we are happy or sad
In the darkness or in the rain
We can see through all our pain
Because we know!
Where the mountainside meets the Sea
Where the eagle flies free
In a large city or down a country lane
God is all… and always He is the same.
Whether alone or in a crowd
With the lowly or the proud
His Church is within us don't you see?
In Spirit and in Truth, in all the beauty that He created for you and for me!
Until we reach heavens shores,
We thank and praise you Lord.
For letting us be here on this beautiful earth you have created
To know you-To feel you-To love you, here and now!
Whether briefly or in a long lifetime
What're you've allowed…
Lord, in Spirit and in Truth,
We Thank You!

A Prayer of the Spirit

The food of my soul is thy sacred heart.
The food of my thought is thy sacred heart.
The food of my strength is thy sacred heart.
Alone, I have nothing.
Alone, I am nothing.
My thoughts and my words and my deeds tell the tale.
The wasted years of my life are hard evidence against me.
With you, my Savior, my Lord and my King,
Through your Sacred Heart, all of my sins before God Almighty vanish as if they
had never been.
His word is truth always.
If I do not accept his truth I am lost.
Therefore are my hands open before you God Almighty Father.
My answer to you is "Yes, I do accept the grace and gift of thy forgiveness"
I loathe my sins and they disgust me.
Only through your Sons shed blood will I endeavor to think on them no more!
My thanks and praise is hardly enough….
And I know too well that all my efforts add up to nothing for what you,
Almighty Father, have done for me through your perfect plan:
To send your only beloved Son to be the sacrificial lamb- for all mankind-
So that we humans, unworthy as we are, my stand before you at the end of time
to be allowed into thy Kingdom.
Through no merit of our own,
You have made your house our home!
Because you love us whom you have made with thy own hand,
And it is by your Word, our Savior, your Son…
That all of this has been done!
Amen

My Praise, My Thanks, My Prayer:

Praise God for the life He has given me. Praise God for the years He has given me. Praise God for all of the mistakes I have made. For every wrong path I ever took. For all the years I wasted, during the years I heeded not His voice, for Almighty God in His Mercy has chosen to turn my mistakes into pure gold! God thank you for my trials and all of my tragedies and thank you and praise you for my sicknesses and pain. Praise you God for letting me live long enough to see you right my wrongs! Praise to you God for the family you have blessed me with. Thank you God for showing me your mercy during all the times I did not deserve your mercy. Thank you God for your forgiveness, for it has freed me to forgive. Praise to you God for all of those who love me and also for those who do not love me. Praise you God for my sister and brothers; my Mother and my Father. Thank you for my precious Sons and for my precious Grandchildren Lord. Thank you for my husband, your servant. Thank you Lord for my beloved Dogs! Praise you God for my heavenly sisters and brothers, my intercessors, your Saints! Praise you for all of your creations! I see your mighty works and it brings me to tears. Praise you God for the humble insect, and for all of the beauty of the animals. Praise you God for the majesty of the trees, the mountains, the Ocean, the night sky, the sunlight, the clouds white and the clouds dark with rain! I love you God for all you have created is very dear to me. Praise you God for anything I suffer. May my suffering be an offering for my dear ones and for those who most need you and for those who need to know and feel your love. May my suffering be an offering for those who do not care for me, as well as for those who have gone before me, those souls most in need. God may all of my suffering be used by you in any way you will, if only as a small token for all you've done for me God. If you give me more time here on Earth I praise you. If you do not give me more time I will live on still, by your mercy, to praise you forever in Heaven. I love you and praise you forever. Amen

Remember

When the doctors tell you "There is no cure", just remember, the doctor is speaking for man. For every single disease on earth there certainly is a cure. There always has been, the cure is Jesus. So, remember if you are a believer and you hear those words "There is no cure", just hear it as, "There is no cure known to man." Know that if you do have any disease, be it large or small, be it painless but bothersome, be it very painful but unseen to the naked eye, your cure is Jesus.

God will have mercy on who He will. If you have prayed and His answer is "No", remember, He has said "No" for your own good. He knows what we do not! He knows how far we can run and how far we can jump. He knows that some people whom he dearly loves, people that he does not want to lose to this world, are better suited not to run and jump. Because He is God; he knows those who would likely run and jump far away from everlasting life. He knows that they would likely run and jump themselves straight into hell.

Some who say they believe but do not accept Gods "No" to them, as pure love, are not listening to His Holy Spirit. Remember that God wants that none should perish, but have life everlasting through Christ Jesus His beloved Son. Yes there is a cure for every disease on earth the cure is certainly Jesus who died on the cross, not only for our sins, our mortal bodies, but, for our immortal souls as well. He died that we, who He loves, may live on earth to produce much fruit for the Kingdom of Heaven. He died that we may live to love our neighbor so much that we desire to snatch them up so they too may spend eternity in Heaven. Remember our purpose here in this life is to radiate Jesus so much so that those who see us want what we have! If you are sick and there is no cure, remember, our neighbors are watching! Do we tell our neighbor that we believe, but curse our conditions in front of them? If we do then we leave them thinking that Jesus is a God of no answers. No we have to praise Him for our sickness, yes, praise Him for our neighbors' sake. For we know without doubt that Jesus loves us.

We know that at His word we are healed. We are healed whether His answer is "yes" or "no". Remember God knows us better than we know ourselves. Therefore His answers are always right and good, and always out of pure love for us.

Good Friday Observations

Do you see your people, oh Lord?

How we long for you.

What ends we fragile humans will go to, just to have you near.

When we lay you before the alter on our Easter time week

There, on the cross….is but an image.

We cry, we pray, we thank you

We touch your image tenderly, only to be with you.

I know our efforts are weak.

But, can anyone say they are altogether useless?

For all that we desire is; to see you.

How can we thank you? We can't.

How can we crucify you over again with our sins? We do.

Please don't look away from your people's efforts, Lord

We were not there to walk with you, the man, all those centuries ago.

But, if we let you, you will live in our hearts and consume our souls!

If we say "yes" we can live with you now, on our earthly journey.

Until at last we realize our promised reward….to see you face to face.

Forever!

Listen

When you hear your name being whispered on the wind
When you hear Him knocking on your heart's door, let Him in
Listen to my song; I wrote it for you friend
Yes, listen and stop the fight.
You know I'm right.
Just let Him in

You see so many things you can't explain
Then you say that you don't care and that you can take the pain.
Your whole life you've been afraid, but you won't admit it.
You see the truth, but turn away.
You say you never did believe all that stuff anyway.
Still, you can't escape, and you complain
When all you need to do is call His name,
But, you're afraid, yes, you are afraid to even say His name!

So listen to my song, I wrote it for you friend.
Yes listen…Stop the fight…You know I'm right.
Just let Him in!
Yeah stop your fight, you know I'm right
Let Him In.

Because of You

Because of You I have no more pain.
Because of You I'm no longer in chains.
My spirit is at peace and so therefore I rest.
I need no longer hide, for Your path it is the best.
I felt the dark of sins knocking at my door,
Then You gave me freedom which made my future sure.
Because of You, Oh Lord, my soul can smile at last.
Because of You, Oh Lord, my soul is no longer masked
By sin and lies and wrong, at long last they are gone!
And to You I belong,
And for You sing my song.

A Wee Praise

I praise you Lord for what green I see
For the soft spring rain that falls on me
For the doves, huddled together under bush and tree
I praise you Lord for all these things!